MW01116438

LLC

Beginner's Guide

2023

The Most Updated Guide on How to Start, Grow, and Run your Single-Member Limited Liability Company.

Thomas Newton

Table of Contents

Introduction

Welcome to the journey of being a part of an LLC. An LLC is a Limited Liability Company. If you pay attention to small businesses, you've probably noticed a lot of company names with LLCs written at the end. An LLC is a business structure that allows individuals to benefit from tax laws while also providing a level of security typically reserved for larger corporations.

The main element that an LLC shares with a corporation are its limited liability components.

It is critical to remember that the formation of an LLC does not imply that the newly formed entity is a corporation; rather, it provides the business structure with some of the benefits that a corporation enjoys.

An LLC is more accurately identified as a voluntary association. A voluntary association sounds self-explanatory but has a deeper meaning, like most business terms. A voluntary association is the formation of a group to achieve specific goals to protect the business members. In the case of an LLC, the goals may be directed toward having a distinct business rather than just a hobby income stream.

Because an LLC is described as a type of association, it has some flexibility. This adaptability is best demonstrated when deciding how to run your business daily. This structure allows each business member to participate in decision-making, or at the very least allows the members to select a member or group to manage the business's operations. It is even possible for someone not part of the managing or executive command structure to run the business.

Unlike other forms of formal business models, individuals involved in an LLC are not required to organize formal meetings or prepare written documentation of the meetings so that they can be reviewed in an audit later.

However, your LLC should hold annual meetings of the board of corporate directors and shareholders.

The decisions made at these meetings should be documented in writing. This is a simple way for those involved in the LLC to protect its members and those with a financial interest in the LLC from personal liability for the professional actions of the business while conducting official business.

Chapter 1. The Benefits of LLC for Small Business Owners

It is no longer a secret that most SMEs prefer an LLC as their business entity. The benefits of an LLC are straightforward, given that multiple factors are critical in forming a limited liability company: the intermediate cost and effort required to continue forming an LLC. But what is the benefit of an LLC for a small business owner?

An LLC can be easily formed privately with minimum expenses by simply locating and adding your company information with template posts. It takes approximately 15 minutes.

Selecting a limited liability company (LLC) as a business structure offers several advantages to all sorts of businesses. Business owners that incorporate as an LLC do so via their state, so the procedures and expenses differ slightly, but the benefits are consistent: personal liability protection, flexibility in operational and taxing structure, and broad eligibility.

Benefits of LLC

Suitable for individuals

The benefits of an LLC are not limited to multi-member businesses. Individuals might also profit from forming a single-member LLC. You receive personal asset protection and more control over how you choose to be taxed. For certain firms, deciding to be taxed as an S corp may result in tax savings; however, state restrictions regarding S corp status differ, and so do your local study.

Personal liability protection

Among the most significant advantages of creating an LLC is that it isolates your personal assets from those of the business. This protects your house, vehicle, and money if your company is sued or fails on a loan.

A personal guarantee for company finance is an exception. That does allow creditors to make you personally liable for debt repayment. Furthermore, if there is proof of fraud or negligence causing injury to people concerned, you might be held personally liable in a lawsuit.

Cheaper & surprisingly simple to form

Starting a business as an LLC is relatively simple and affordable compared to corporations. The particular procedure is controlled by your state, although the paperwork and expense are usually modest. In addition to completing a brief formation document, you'll need to file articles of organization and an operating agreement explaining the new company's ownership structure. Templates for them may be accessible online, so you don't have to start from scratch.

Because of the lower operational complexity, incorporating an LLC is typically more enticing to small firms than founding a corporation. LLCs are not obligated to have an annual shareholders' meeting or file an annual report.

Pliable Taxation

Selecting an LLC as your entity type provides you with several possibilities for paying taxes. Only if an LLC elects to be taxed as C corporation profits are passed through to the owners as personal income rather than corporate taxes, this is known as pass-through taxes, and it saves money by avoiding double taxation (at the corporate level and the personal level).

But, depending on your tax categorization, you may be required to pay self-employment taxes.

The QBI (qualified business income) deduction, a recent tax law modification, also enables many LLCs to qualify for a Federal Tax Deduction on pass-through revenue. Business owners with pass-through income can deduct up to 20% of their net income on their federal tax returns until 2025.

Flexibility in ownership and management

Members of an LLC company structure can decide how earnings are distributed. In contrast, a general partnership compels all partners to divide corporate earnings equally. Instead, LLCs allow earnings to be divided according to the operating agreement's provisions. If one member puts in more money upfront or more sweat equity (performing the hard work of bringing the firm to maturity), the agreement may offer them a bigger share of the earnings.

Furthermore, the number of owners in an LLC is not restricted. There is also no necessity for a governing body, such as a board of directors or a group of executives, as a corporation would.

Using a Demand Letter to Benefit Your LLC

Are you familiar with a letter of request and how your company can benefit from it? When you form an LLC, you ensure that every customer pays every bill on time. When you form an LLC, any customers will simply refuse to pay. However, before going to court, try writing a letter outlining your request. This will help you get the desired results while saving money and time. Demand letters assist in resolving 30% of all future conflicts between LLCs and other companies. The beauty of a letter of request is that it is inexpensive and simple to write; it is a simple, concise letter requesting payment. If the consumer does not pay or no agreement is reached, you will have additional paperwork to present to a court.

People do not expect a small company owner to tackle the debt with the same rigor as a big company. Thus, they will sadly neglect your polite attempts to obtain payments. A letter from your LLC states why you owe, what you owe, and the legal alternative if you don't pay. This shows that you are serious and willing to appear before the court. Sometimes, the prospect of appearing before the judge and facing your debt publicly is enough to make people pay; however, you want to avoid court as much as possible.

The best way to represent your LLC is through a well-written letter. To make the request letter successful, you want to include a few main items:

- A debt history. While the client should know why it owes it and the efforts you have made to recover it, it does provide a comprehensive history for the judge if you must go to court.
- Enter the unique results you are looking for. E.g., '$250.00 must be completely paid on or before July 1.'
- Professional look and sound. Your letter of request represents your LLC. Type a letter on the letterhead of the company. Avoid misrepresentation and keep the content company linked. Retain a copy of your documents.
- Conclude your letter by stating that you intend to take legal action if your request is not fulfilled. E.g., "If the full amount is not paid before July 1, $250 will be added to the amount immediately."

In an ideal world, you provide good products, and, in return, the customer pays promptly. If that does not apply to your situation, consider submitting a request letter and utilizing your valuable time to run your LLC.

An Explanation of LLCs & Disadvantages

Limited Liability Companies or LLCs are among the most common company forms for entrepreneurs who start new projects. If you have ever looked at the names of companies selling products and services, some of them may have corporate names that end in "LLC." An LLC is a company type. If you've ever considered starting your own business, this is one of your options. However, before registering your business in this manner, you should learn more about LLCs to determine whether they are the right type of company for you.

The founders of the LLC, also known as "members," are not directly responsible for the company's debts and costs. You may ask, "But don't other business types, like corporations, have this form of protection?" Yes, other business types may provide limited liability to you, but the LLC has other advantages.

To begin with, it's very easy to create. Most states have forms that you can only download if you send them in. Your pay fees are usually negligible in most countries (unless you want to process them quickly). In the long run, the records and documents required by LLCs are usually simpler.

With LLC, you can vote for taxes. You could choose to be taxed as a partnership, S Company, or C Company. This flexibility is attractive for many business owners, especially those who want to profit from cheaper taxes.

You don't have to worry about double taxation when it comes to taxes unless you choose to be taxed as a C Corporation or form your LLC in the District of Columbia. You are only charged with the same salary once. This benefit makes LLC an enticing option for people who run a freelance or consulting enterprise.

Even with its numerous benefits, an LLC still has a few disadvantages. One big downside is that you cannot sell the company's stocks or shares. This makes expanding difficult, especially for companies that expect to be published one day. Furthermore, if one owner wishes to leave the company, the LLC and the remaining owners must be dissolved. If they want to continue operating together, the LLC must be reformed again.

The LLC is also a new organization. As a result, it lacks the reputation of trust associated with a company or other type of enterprise. This makes finding capital more difficult if you are looking for external investors. This also means that national laws on LLCs vary because there is no agreement on how the government should handle them fiscally and administratively.

As you can see, LLCs have perks and drawbacks like any other company structure. The business owner decides if the benefits of creating an LLC are worth the disadvantages you face.

Chapter 2. How to Start an LLC

A Limited Liability Company, as opposed to a sole proprietorship or corporation, provides additional legal protection. They usually stand out from their owners.

Filing as an LLC requires additional steps and documentation, which vary by state. You may be charged a fee to send these documents. Although forming an LLC takes more time and money, it provides greater security, which you may want in the event of an accident.

An organization, like an LLC, needs paperwork detailing people's positions within the business. Corporations comprise stockholders who own the company, directors who control it, and officers who manage its day-to-day operations.

Your company would typically need to apply bylaws and articles of incorporation to register as a corporation, but the exact requirements vary by state. Corporations are taxed differently than other types of businesses.

Corporations are the most complex entity in terms of legal work, but they also have the most security. A corporation may be the best option if you have multiple owners or expect significant growth.

Steps in Forming LLC

One of the most significant stages in starting a business is forming a limited liability company (LLC). An LLC can provide your company with liability protection in addition to other benefits. In contrast, the specific procedures for forming an LLC vary substantially by state. Following are some basic guidelines about what to expect throughout the procedure.

Select a State

LLCs can be incorporated in any 50 states, irrespective of where you live or want to do business. Among the fifty states, Delaware, Nevada, and Wyoming laws are among the most business-friendly. Income earned outside of Delaware is not subject to taxation in that state. Business income is not taxed in Nevada or Wyoming. A first-time business owner will frequently select one of these three states when incorporating an LLC.

However, evading the taxman is not so simple. If you incorporate in any of these states, there is a good probability that you will wind up paying more overall.

If business companies could evade business income taxes simply by incorporating Nevada or Wyoming, everyone would do so.

We strongly advise creating your LLC in your native state.

There are three main reasons why you should avoid incorporating your new LLC outside of your native state:

- You'll still have to pay your home state taxes.
- You will have to pay twice for registered agents, annual filings, franchise taxes, and other expenses.
- It's simply inconvenient.

Naming your LLC

As you evaluate business names, marketing may be at the forefront of your mind. While picking the proper name for branding considerations is critical, your business name must also comply with state legislation. Find a name that makes sense for your company.

In any case, you may always register a DBA, sometimes called a Fictitious Business Name (FBA). DBAs enable you to use any name as your trade name.

Your LLC name remains the same as a DBA, but your brand name might differ.

Prerequisites for Naming

State regulations differ significantly. However, the respective standards are universal:

- It must be a distinct name.

- The phrase "LLC," "Limited Liability Company," or "Ltd." must be included.
- It cannot include terms or phrases that may be mistaken with government agencies, such as the Police Department, IRS, Department of State, etc.
- It cannot contain protected terms like "college," "hospital," or "bank" unless there is a compelling cause to do so.

Select a Registered Agent

You need to have a registered agent, either an individual or a business, to act as the official contact for your limited liability company.

Official communication and service of process (legal papers connected to litigation) will always be sent to the postal address of your registered agent by government entities and attorneys.

Individuals over 18 can be registered agents if they have a physical address in the state where your LLC was created. Companies can also be registered agents.

You can legally appoint yourself as your LLC's registered agent.

We highly advise you not to appoint yourself.

The registered agent information is open to the public and may be seen online. If you value your privacy, never appoint yourself.

It is best to choose a third party as your registered agent. That third party is typically a legal firm or a registered agent service.

Typically, registered agent businesses charge around $120 per year to act as your registered agent. Attorneys frequently charge extra, sometimes up to $500 per year.

File Articles of Organization

You will be required to submit papers to the state agency that handles company filings in your state to create your LLC as a legal organization. When you file articles of formation with your Secretary of State, your limited liability corporation is legally constituted. In certain states, these articles are also called a certificate of formation or a certificate of organization.

Documents required for formation must include:

- The LLC's business address
- The LLC's registered agent's name and address
- The founding member's name & address details

- Whether your LLC is administered by members or by non-members
- Effective date
- Validity of your LLC, if you wish it to expire at a specific date
- Business Purpose Statement

The articles can be filed by mail or online. The actual filing fee will differ from state to state. When submitting this document, you must supply accurate information.

Online formation providers manage the full LLC creation or incorporation procedure from beginning to end. It's the easiest and quickest approach to establishing a limited liability company. Since they handle everything digitally, they may save money by filing everything themselves rather than hiring an attorney or certified public accountant.

Draft an Operating Agreement

If you are creating your own limited liability company (LLC), the operating agreement is the single most crucial document. It establishes the ground principles for how your organization operates internally and with the public. As a result, ensuring that your business structure works for you is critical.

Although most states do not require LLCs to have operating agreements, having one is vital to get your firm off to a good start and offer it the best chance of success.

A limited liability company's objective is to protect your personal assets. Personal assets such as automobiles, residences, and money are not in danger if your company is sued or goes bankrupt.

Furthermore, without personal liability protection, your company organization is more akin to a sole proprietorship, which means creditors can seize your personal assets. The end effect might be disastrous for both your business and your life.

The LLC operating agreement explicitly states your, the other LLC members, and the company's connection. It guarantees that the LLC company structure fully protects you and the other members and that the firm functions smoothly.

Operating agreements provide these safeguards in a variety of ways:

- They define the rights and responsibilities of LLC members. The operating agreement for a limited liability company should state whether or not a single member of the LLC is responsible for day-to-day operations and record keeping.

- What is a non-member manager permitted to accomplish? Managers are held to higher standards of accountability by the company and its members. The operating agreement is where these details can be laid down.

- What the LLC is lawfully entitled to. The operating agreement should also specify how the company may perform its operations daily.

- How new employees can join the organization. They also set guidelines for how an LLC member can depart.

- When and how revenues are distributed to members. They can also design various forms of membership and payment programs.

- Whether members or management in charge, they also guide how to hire and terminate managers.

- How and under what conditions should the LLC be terminated? You may not wish to dissolve your company right now, but you may in the future. It's wise to think about it and plan ahead of time before it becomes a problem.

- How to Modify the Rules In the future, you may need to revise your LLC operating agreement. The operating agreement should specify how adjustments will be made.

When you look at the laws of most states, you'll see that they frequently have their own "default" regulations for how these things work in an LLC. In most circumstances, operating agreements allow you to tailor the regulations to your own scenario.

If you do not have an LLC operating agreement and something unexpected occurs, the future of your LLC may be determined by what state legislation is in effect at the time. With your contract in place, you get control of your firm and its destiny.

Putting together an operating agreement may be daunting. The easiest way to go about it is to consult a lawyer or business formation agency about your company's requirements.

Obtain an EIN

An Employer Identification Number (EIN) is your LLC's nine-digit tax identification number. Consider it your LLC's social security number. The IRS uses these numbers to maintain track of business organizations for tax purposes.

The government requires EINs for any LLCs that produce money or wish to hire staff. Most financial institutions require an EIN when opening a business bank account.

You must submit an EIN application to the IRS. Applications can be submitted using the SS-4 form via mail or online. Once completing the online form, you will get EIN instantly.

An EIN is not required for single-member LLCs. You can substitute your social security number. However, we strongly advise having an EIN to protect your identity and separate your personal and corporate funds.

LLC as an Individual

A person with CLL is someone who wishes to form an LLC. It is a hybrid business structure that shares characteristics with both a corporation and a sole proprietorship. Its owners, like those of a corporation, have personal protection. The company's debts do not affect its assets. Profits and losses are declared in the income tax declaration for the sole owner in the same way for single ownership.

A sole proprietorship is a business owned and operated by a single individual. The default is unique if it does not act as a Limited Liability Company or Corporation and does not have a single owner. As previously stated, all gains, losses, expenses, and business deductions are reported on the owner's tax return because the company does not pay corporate tax.

The Rules of a Single Member LLC

The Limited Liability Corporation may be a perplexing business structure as an appealing association. A few significant differences distinguish the LLC from the standard (or limited liability) format.

Individual LLC members are distinguished from ordinary LLCs because the former has only one member, owner, or manager. The technological gap closes here, but there are a few other possibilities.

Note: Not all states will allow you to join a single LLC member. You will be asked to form a sole proprietorship that you form instead. This is unfortunate because it limits limited liability rights. It is, however, a factor. The good news is that you do not have to live in a state to organize your company (you simply want to do business there), so your geographical location is not an impediment. For example, you could live in Nevada and form an LLC in Delaware, similar to how the company does.

A Risky Endeavor

Unfortunately, because LLCs (i.e., partnerships) exist, some of the benefits of LLCs are not usually realized by their members. Many legal professionals would allow you to establish a relationship with your organization even if you only give a close family member or friend 2% of your business. This is due to several complex rules and laws.

Charge Order Protection

The government forbids your creditors from seizing corporate assets to protect them. Rather, you can only demand your share of the Company's income. You create this complex by constructing an SMLLC. As a result, you can avoid this by filling out IRS Form 8832 and electing to have your company taxed as a corporation.

Death and Operating Agreements

As a sole member of an LLC, the organization is subject to several restrictions (partly because this type of business has emerged as an alternative to a partnership). A significant but often overlooked advantage of businesses is that their lives are unrelated to the lives or well-being of a single person. When an owner (stockholder) passes away, the company simply redistributes its ownership and continues to operate.

Multi-partner LLCs operate in the same way that regular LLCs do, but single LLCs do not. In this case, the operating contract must specify who will take over ownership in the event of the owner's death. The individuals will usually support this.

Tax Time

Single LLCs also have their own set of tax rules. The IRS regards the arrangement as an unrecognized entity and taxes LLCs with one owner in the same way it charges sole property.

As always, take notes and keep your personal and business finances separate. This is true for all organizations, but it is especially important when shaping and operating an LLC as a single member of complicated situations.

Although many people do not recommend operating as a single LLC member, other types of activity are possible and potentially better. Always keep track of the complicated state of affairs as you work and brace yourself (or the will) for a headache.

Start-Up Choice: Corporation Inc or LLC?

LLC Vs. Partnership

This association article refers to two business entities: a Limited Liability Company and a partnership. While they are similar legal forms, they differ in personal responsibility, management controls, formal processes, and other features.

Association Against LLC: Differences and Similarities

A Limited Liability Company (LLC) is a popular business entity that shares characteristics with other legal structures known as partnerships. They are similar in terms of how they were formed and the "pass-through" method of taxation, but they differ in terms of characteristics such as participant responsibility.

What is an Association?

An Association is a kind of business with many partners who are necessarily co-owners. To form a company:

- You must have 2 or more parties agree to have the company operate for profit.
- Partners share management activities and share gains and financial losses of the company.
- The amount of income depends on the individual owner's initial investment.

Several partnerships exist, depending on the industry and the owners' desires.

Forming an LLC entails registering the business in the state where it is located as a partnership. Most Limited

Liability Companies operate based on an operating agreement, which specifies the percentage of questions from members and answers to "what if?" questions. An LLC is a taxation by-pass style of a partnership or sole proprietorship that lacks the benefit of personal responsibility and is as limited as a society.

Personal, Limited Liability

Personal, Limited Liability means its owners divide their assets and judgments against the company. The owners' personal property, such as a car or home, cannot be touched by creditors if the company receives a lawsuit or a debt that jeopardizes the organization. Owners' illegal, unethical, or reckless behavior results in the cancellation of the limited liability protection.

Many people consider the LLC format an ideal combination of a partnership and a corporation, given its distinguishing characteristics. It is a hybrid corporate-individual business structure.

Chapter 3.   Is an LLC Right for Me?

The decision to form an LLC or take your business in another direction could be the key to your company's success. Legalzoom.com stated, "When an owner establishes the LLC, startup costs are low, and there is less paperwork than there is when starting a corporation. If an LLC is properly operated, and its assets and agreements are in the business's name, the members will not be personally liable for the actions and debts of the business."

This is a compelling reason a company should consider incorporating it as an LLC. One of the most important reasons to form an LLC is to protect yourself and your family from some financial risks associated with running a business.

One of the advantages of forming an LLC as the owner or founder of the company is that the initial startup costs are low. Another advantage of forming an LLC is that significantly less paperwork is required than forming a corporation. It is critical to ensure that your LLC is properly managed.

This ensures that your business and its assets and agreements are in the business's name. The proper operation and filing of the essential paperwork will allow your members to not be personally liable for the actions and debts of the business. These are some of the benefits of forming an LLC.

While there aren't many disadvantages to running your business as an LLC, it's important to understand that some obligations may not be the best fit for your company or your expectations of what an LLC can do for you. Some of the components of an LLC that must be fully considered include the fact that there will be ongoing expenses to maintain the LLC.

These costs, however, will apply to other types of business structures, such as corporations and partnerships. Even if taxes on the LLC's income are often passed through to the individual members, the LLC must still file tax returns.

One advantage that may be important to your business is that the owners of an LLC are not required to reside in the United States. When forming an LLC, there is no legal residency requirement. If you are not a citizen or permanent resident of the United States, this could be another plus in your favor when deciding whether an LLC is right for your business.

The ability to remain an LLC, relocate outside of the United States, or have members of your LLC located in or from various parts of the world may be the best fit for your company, especially if your business caters to non-U.S. citizen-clients.

The credibility that comes with becoming an LLC is one of the less tangible factors that must be considered when deciding whether you want or need to form your business into a legally recognized business. When a company applies for or becomes an official business entity, it can positively impact how others perceive your company.

Taking the time and spending money to form an LLC demonstrates that your business is a serious entity, not a side project. Vendors, suppliers, and other professional services contractors will be less wary of doing business with a company that appears to take its responsibilities seriously. The organization's owners and members have taken responsible precautions to protect themselves.

Your potential and current customers, like your vendors, may be concerned about the legitimacy of your company. Customers are more likely to trust your company if they believe you and your company are fully invested in your product or service. Customers are sold on your confidence by displaying that your company is an LLC.

Another disadvantage of forming an LLC is that ownership in an LLC is often more difficult to transfer than in other business structures, such as a corporation. This gives all members of the LLC, regardless of their ownership stake in the company, a similar amount of power when it comes to adding new members to the LLC.

The most significant disadvantage of forming an LLC is reducing the growth potential. Every year, many business owners strive to expand their operations and achieve greater levels of success. An LLC limits this growth for some business models because it does not allow for the distribution of shares in the LLC to attract potential investors.

While this is a significant disadvantage for some business owners considering incorporating their company as an LLC, it is not always a deal-breaker. It could be an option if your company is new and in its early stages. Creating a new legal structure for your company is always possible, but this is a time-consuming and costly process.

The LLC structure is a newer business model in the United States. This novelty generates an interesting debate as to whether it is positive or negative. This is because the court system has yet to rule on some issues that may arise with your LLC. This is not a major concern for your company at this time, as the benefits of an LLC outweigh the potential risk of entering an area of the legal system where some of the gray areas of operating an LLC have not yet been fully resolved.

It is best to take your time in the early stages of determining which path is right for your company. Making a list of your company's goals can help you decide what legal structure will work best for you in the short and long term.

Consulting with a corporate lawyer about your plans is never a bad idea. However, this is not always necessary. Joining a local small business owners' group is another excellent source of information and support. There, you will be able to discuss the benefits and drawbacks of your company, as well as what types of corporate structures will work best for you.

Odds are your business will benefit from becoming an LLC, but make sure that you and your partners have taken the appropriate due diligence to ensure that you are doing what is best for your business, yourself, and your partners.

What's the Difference Between a Business's Legal Structure and Tax Structure?

- The tax structure is handled by the IRS on a federal basis, while your state handles the company structure.
- The IRS does not accept LLCs, even though you register as one with the department. You may be classified as a sole proprietor, partnership, S-corporation, or C-corporation for tax purposes.
- Under the LLC, you will get all the defense advantages, but the tax process differs.
- You can save money on FICA (Federal Insurance Contributions Act) payments, also known as payroll taxes, and escape double taxation by forming an S-corporation.

The company owner usually shapes the company with dire tax implications without consulting an experienced company or a tax consultant. Even the NYS State Division of Companies Website mentions this fact: "Therefore, it is advisable to review, with a close look at the tax consequences, the business situation when deciding which organization to form."

In fact, many LLCs have been created for the wrong reasons, with catastrophic consequences for companies and their owners who will bear the burden of that decision for years to come and probably decades to come.

A Limited Liability Company is the combination of a company and a partnership. They closely mimic and are taxed like partnerships but are limited liability benefits like companies.

They are established by registering a unique name through the secretary of state in the state where the company is located. Each state has its particular rules and fee schedules for forming one. The cost of establishing an LLC in NYS is considerably more due to the need to publish a notice of intent.

An LLC is formed by paying a fee and filing articles of the organization with the appropriate state office. It can be established in several states by filing a simple one-page document that sets out the LLC's Articles of Organization. The new LLC must choose a name, a place for its headquarters, and the names of all of its founding members. Some states will also require LLCs to announce the business's expected duration, file an operating agreement, and provide other legally required details. Annual fees and filing requirements are also common.

Some corporations, such as banks and insurance companies, cannot be LLC, just as they cannot be an S company. Unlike an S corporation, however, an LLC may have members that are corporations, associations, or even foreign organizations (there are some special rules for foreign-owned LLCs). In addition, unlike an S company, the number of owners/members of the business is unrestricted. Most states recognize them as separate entity forms for tax purposes, but the federal government does not recognize them as such. As a result, it may specify how it wants to be handled by the IRS for tax purposes. The IRS will treat an LLC with one member (or a single-member LLC) as a sole proprietorship for tax purposes unless otherwise stated, and the IRS will "disregard" it as an entity form. An LLC disregarded object is what this is called. This ignored status has no bearing on liability protection; it simply instructs the IRS and the taxpayer that taxes should be charged as though they did not exist. By default, the IRS can consider an LLC with more than one member (or a multi-member LLC) as a partnership. An IRS Form 8832 should be filed if it wishes to be treated as a C company. If there is some doubt on how the IRS will handle it for tax purposes, Form 8832 allows the LLC to designate how the company should be taxed directly. A company, association, sole proprietor, disregarded entity, domestic entity, or international entity are the choices available on that form. However, the LLC must meet the prerequisite conditions for becoming an S corporation, which includes filing Form 8832 and opting to be treated as a corporation.

Converting business forms necessitates some advanced legal and tax research, which you can do with the assistance of an attorney and accountant.

The person from whom you want to be treated as within your LLC determines the IRS taxation rules you must obey on a federal level. If you don't make a selection and have a single-member LLC, you'll be subject to the sole proprietor/self-employed taxation laws, and if you have a multiple-member LLC, you'll be subject to the general partnership taxation rules.

To ensure that it receives the proper tax treatment, you must file IRS Form 8832, which specifies the tax treatment for your LLC. Suppose you want to be categorized as an S corporation. In that case, you must first choose to be "listed as an organization taxable as a corporation" on IRS Form 8832 and then apply IRS Form 2553 to specify further that you want to be treated as an S corporation. These are time-sensitive documents, so send them as soon as possible to ensure IRS acceptance of your chosen selection.

Chapter 4.   LLC: Incorporating Success in Your Business

By forming an LLC, industries ranging from real estate to construction will reap numerous benefits and provide the company and its customers with more opportunities.

When establishing a company, an LLC is a company structure that allows your company to have legal liability similar to that of a corporation while avoiding annual reports, share distributions, regulations, and other requirements.

Forming an LLC is especially advantageous for new businesses. It combines a relationship's control and tax advantages with the least amount of transparency. Members of an LLC are frequently protected from corporate liability or lawsuits. An LLC is more adaptable than a corporation because its members can include foreign individuals, trusts, associations, businesses, and non-residents. Furthermore, maintenance is simple; an LLC has fewer formalities and is easier to operate than a corporation.

Variations in the LLC Relative to the Business

- Companies are owned by ownership shares or inventories that are distributed to shareholders. Like partnerships, an LLC belongs to its members or managers.
- In comparison to LLC, businesses need annual meetings and written minutes. LLC requires less paperwork because these standards do not apply.
- A company must pay income taxes on its earnings at the corporate tax rate. An LLC is a "pass-through" tax agency, on the other hand. The gains or losses

generated by the corporation shall appear on the owners' income tax returns. Therefore, the double taxation of corporate and personal income tax payable is avoided.

What to Expect After Filing An LLC

Once you have opted to apply for an LLC, the paperwork will be clarified in two articles with a CD. They will come along with the corporate or LLC pack.

The Organizational Articles formalize your life by following the laws of the state. After you've filed this, you'll have a legal company up and running.

This document specifies the company's name, intent, incorporators, quantities, stock types that may be issued, and any other unique characteristics. On the other hand, the operating agreement includes the LLC's written code of conduct. Meetings, board and officer appointments, notices, forms and duties, and a standard procedure are required.

There will also be a registered agent who can accept official documents on your behalf. Examples of documents received are tax advisories, annual reports, and documents relating to the legal process, such as appeals.

The final steps include submitting an amendment article to reflect the shift of your business from a company to an LLC. You must also submit an original or annual report. Experts in business filing may assist in the processing of required business changes.

Choice of Business Entity

The most common type of corporation is an LLC. Because most small and medium-sized businesses are best organized as a corporation or Limited Liability Companies, this article focuses on the fundamental similarities and differences. I attempted to provide a synopsis of the following key elements. However, keep in mind that the following information will not allow you to make an informed decision about a person. This can all be accomplished with the help of a lawyer and an accountant.

C Corporation

The largest firms are C firms. C Companies are all publicly traded companies. The term "C" is taken from the Internal Revenue Code, Subchapter C, which controls corporate taxes. There are some reasons why C businesses are more appropriate for large firms. Multiple stock groups, infinite number and shareholder forms, a fiscal year versus a calendar tax year, and corporate profit retention are just some of the major differences of a C Company. This is generally ideal for companies that want publicly to raise capital or whose class of investors differs.

Most notably, double taxation extends to C Companies. This means that all of the profits of the C Company are once taxed at the corporate level, and then the same income is taxed again at the shareholder level when the benefit is a dividend. Double taxation can sometimes be avoided in smaller C Companies by annually abolishing net profits by paying shareholder workers. Shareholders must declare any dividend earnings as capital gains on their tax returns.

For tax purposes, a business begins as a C Business. Unless the shareholder elects "S" corporate tax status, as discussed below, all companies will be known as C Corporations by default. The corporation's net profits (after deducting pay, company expenses, and furniture and equipment depreciation) are net. The C

Corporation will only be taxed on "effectively related" revenue from a corporate tax rate of 15% on the first $50,000 taxable income per year.

When the organization is listed as a "Personal Service Business" (PSC), a flat fee of 35 percent from the dollar of a net profit would be charged. This is a typically unwanted form of entity. The CSPs are companies whose owners operate in accounting, acting, architectural, technological, health and veterinary services, law, and performance services. The lowest tax rate of 15 percent is only possible for a business that offers personal services if the company does not employ and hold at least 6 percent of its issued stock. Otherwise, the highest personal tax rate will apply to personal service taxable income in that business. A PSC is, by definition, a C organization. A timely S-election will negate your Company's classification as a PSC and escape the 35% flat tax rate.

The use of a C Corporation results in some special tax advantages. One of the most significant advantages for SMEs is the ability to deduct all health insurance premiums paid by employed owners and their spouses and dependents. Furthermore, a C Corporation may enact a MERP (medical, dental, and drug expenses refund plan) at any time during the fiscal year, which can be easily applied back to the beginning of the fiscal year, and can purchase disability insurance for one or more of its managers or other workers. An organization can also exclude disability insurance premiums without affecting the executive's or employee's taxable expenses. Finally, contributions to eligible pension programs will be deducted by an employer.

In terms of ownership, the company is held by shareholders under the company's ownership of stock (or shares). Corporations issue their shareholders' stock certificates to show their ownership percentage. C Companies can have different asset groups, such as common and preferred stocks, offering shareholders different dividends and voting rights. Without affecting the company, shares can be freely exchanged or redeemed. According to Illinois law, like every other Jurisdiction, corporate shareholders typically have a full liability shield from the actions or omissions of the company. The shareholders elect a board of directors who oversee the company's operations and businesses. The law of Illinois requires the appointment of a President, Secretary, and Treasurer, while sole shareholder companies are allowed.

The corporation's bylaws are its guiding text. The bylaws regulate the business and affairs of the company (C and S Companies) and define the board of directors amounts, powers, and obligations, the shareholder's voting rights, the company's dissolution, annual meetings, special meetings, and other corporation rules. Generally, a stock buying/stock restraint contract or similar agreement regulates the relationship between the owners (shareholders) of a small or closely held company. This instrument can provide for buying and selling rights of shareholders, restrictions on the sale or transfer of shares, and purchase rights for companies, among other items. Corporations shall have a collection of bylaws regulating the company in all jurisdictions, or the corporation shall be subject to the default rules set out in the State statute.

Notice that the corporation owners (shareholders) arrangement may also be subject to a separate instrument, such as an inventory purchase or an agreement on inventory restriction, shareholder agreement, or similar document. In general, this document governs the transfer and acquisition of stocks, companies, and/or shareholders.

C Corporation is ideally suited to active companies with a chance of appreciating and high share potential. C businesses typically keep their profits in the early stages of growth and do not share corporate income with shareholders to enjoy it.

S Corporation

S Corporation is a lot like C Company. Its owners are similarly shielded from personal responsibility for the actions or omissions of the companies.

The key difference lies in the S corporation's tax treatment. As suggested, C Companies are taxable at the corporate level, and shareholders are taxed from the same revenue stream as paid as dividends. S Companies, by comparison, prevent dual taxation since only individual owners are taxed. The status of a company is achieved by electing such organizational tax treatment (IRS Form 2553). Net profit, including wages paid to workers and shareholder-employees, after expenses incurred for S companies is declared in federal Form 1120S and transferred to shareholders' tax return through Schedule K-1, where the return is subject to the regular tax. In addition, pass-through losses are restricted to the taxpayer's basis in the S Company stock.

All salaries are taxed on self-employment (payroll). S Companies shall pay shareholder-employee fair wages in exchange for the services the employee gives to the company before non-wage distribution to the shareholder-employee can be made. The S Company pays the employer's share of FICA tax (7.65%), and the employee pays the balance of the FICA tax (7.65%). For the S Company and the shareholder, salaries are subject to a cumulative payroll tax of approximately 15.3 percent plus the shareholder's income tax rate. So, the shareholder-employee can only pay a minimum wage to himself to minimize taxes on the profit stream of businesses. IRS regulations specify that the shareholder-employee be paid fair compensation (many consider this failure to cause an internal audit). However, any other income avoids self-employment taxation and is either subject to ordinary income or capital gains. This means that payroll taxes can only be levied on the fair salaries of employee-holders, not the distributions of the S business.

When do you have to pay salaries? According to the IRS, the shareholder-employee shall assess fair compensation for the S Company. The IRS shall investigate the source of the gross receipts of the S Company:

1. Shareholder services.
2. Non-shareholder staff services.
3. Capital and equipment.

If the gross receipts and income are obtained from things 2 and 3, the shareholder-employee shall be paid no compensation. However, if the bulk of gross sales and income are related to the shareholder's services, part of the profit allocation should be distributed as compensation. (Of course, you can seek more information from an accountant).

Individual owners can still be charged even if profits are not allocated to the owners and are left as working capital. This is because all revenue is distributed directly to shareholders. C-corporation owners are only liable for the dividend taxes they currently collect (although the corporation's undistributed revenue is exempt from self-employment tax).

The disadvantages of the S election position are that the S Company holders to whom they pay the deductions on life benefits, disability insurance, car and life, drug, and dental insurance plans will be taxable.

S Corporations, among other things, are less adaptable than C Corporations and LLCs. Only a few shareholders are allowed; individuals and no foreign shareholders are usually permitted. Small and closely-held businesses that do not intend to publicly raise large sums of capital are generally better suited in this context. In the case of a C venture, the shareholders own the company through their stock in the company. However, unlike a C Corporation, there can only be one type of distribution rights stock.

Corporations typically have low debt, low risk, and a low chance of major appreciation for active companies, as all corporate profits normally are allocated to shareholders.

Limited Liability Company (LLC)

An LLC provides the same personal liability shield that a company offers to its shareholders. However, it offers great flexibility in dealing with capital contributions and allocating gains and losses to shareholders. An LLC will allocate income as it sees fit for its members. For example, assume that you and your partner have an LLC to which you contributed $80,000 of capital and only $20,000 from your partner. If your partner works 80%, the owners will still decide to share the 50/50 profits. However, if you and your partner were shareholders in an S firm, you would have to allocate 80% and 20% to your partner under the statute. If you have any partners, this can be an unfair way to organize your company.

The LLC is taxed as a partnership, as gains and expenses are passed on to the members, and no income tax is charged at the corporate level. The LLC prohibits double taxation, much as the S business does. (Again, some states levy LLC income substitution taxes). The income of the LLC is shown in Form 1065, then distributed via Schedule K-1 to the owners. The owners then record their income (1040) on Schedule E. If the LLC has only one owner, then the IRS considers the LLC automatically as a single owner ("unregarded entity"). A neglected individual does not file a tax return, and the owner declares the profits in compliance with Schedule C of its return. The IRS will immediately handle the LLC as though it were a partnership if the LLC has multiple owners. However, an LLC is a 'check the box' company, which means it may choose to be taxed as a corporation.

There is a lot of misunderstanding regarding self-employment taxes for LLC members. The disparity in your treatment as a general partner and a limited partner, in general, is important in the calculation of self-employment tax liability since an LLC is taxed as a partnership. If a member of an LLC is regarded as a limited partner, the member's share of LLC profits does not have a self-employment tax (except for all guaranteed payments). If a Member is a general partner, they must pay tax on all LLC incomes for self-employment. However, under Section 11402(a)-2 of 1997 Proposed IRS Treasury Regulations, if an LLC member has the authority or provides more than 500 hours per year of service to an LLC of being directly liable for any debt, that member shall, as the general partner, be taxed and shall have a self-employment tax duty on his LLC revenue allocation. Otherwise, the member will be charged as a limited partner and does not have tax responsibilities relating to its LLC revenue allocations for self-employment.

The LLC may also have two interest groups, one of which is treated as a general partnership interest and one as a limited partner interest. If a spouse or member owns both classes of interest, the member may divide the income share between the two classes and pay self-employment taxes on the general partner side but not the restricted partner side. The IRS never formally enforced the draft Regulations for 1997, but many practitioners and taxpayers relied on them. Furthermore, IRS officials have now confirmed that they can rely on it.

Both benefits and losses allocated to members and "salaries" (usually guaranteed payments) paid to them shall be called independent jobs and subject to self-employment taxes. LLC owners are deemed self-employed and must pay a 15.3 percent self-employment fee. Note that only wages are subject to job taxes and not distributions to shareholders in an S Company. The S Company thus gives its shareholders substantial job tax benefits compared to the LLC.

LLCs provide limited liability insurance if properly formed and maintained in most cases, but there are typically few tax advantages to the corporate partnership over the sole proprietorship. The ability of members to limit the transfer of a membership interest to only economic interest is a significant advantage of LLCs over corporations. This means prospective members will only collect dividends (and pay taxes) but have no voting or management rights. If a business shareholder transfers its stock, all ownership attributes, including voting rights, must be transferred unless the stock is non-voting.

The owners of LLCs are called shareholders, and each member has an interest in the business as a percentage of the LLC. LLCs can establish different groups of membership interests similar to C corporations. Members include companies and other LLCs, which provide this organization with ultimate flexibility in its ownership structure. An LLC is typically operated by its members, where the LLC's company and operations are operated by its members themselves, or where either a Member Manager or a foreign manager is named. Members commonly control LLCs. Illinois provides one-member LLCs, like most other nations, if not all. Unlike several other jurisdictions, Illinois requires licensed service providers, such as lawyers and physicians, to create LLCs for business operations.

The Operating Agreement serves as the LLC's guiding document. It is the same as corporate regulation in effectively regulating the same aspects. Most jurisdictions, however, state the contents required in bylaws and operating agreements, and there are, of course, differences. The operating agreement frequently specifies the relationship between the members of an LLC. At the same time, companies typically use various instruments for some shareholder rights, such as stock transfer and buy-out rights of companies.

Real estate investments and companies holding other properties that typically expose their owners to liability risks are generally suitable for LLCs. If you have one or more partners and want flexibility in how the organization distributes benefits (and losses) to its members, the LLC is likely to be the right option.

Chapter 5. What Can a Limited Liability Company Offer to a Small Business?

Companies that Profit from the LLC Structure

In general, LLCs are best suited for:

Organizations with few active shareholders. When there are no more than about 35 owners, the practicalities of making joint choices on the company's direction may be easily managed.

New small businesses. New enterprises typically want to pass on early-year losses to shareholders to deduct against other revenue (Typically, salary obtained while working for another firm or investment income).

Whoever is considering establishing an S-Corporation. S companies, like LLCs, provide all owners with limited liability protection and allow income and losses to be taxed at individual shareholder rates. However, as we'll see in "S corporations," these advantages come at a steep cost: S companies are extremely restricted, and a company might lose eligibility inadvertently—for example, when an ineligible shareholder inherits or purchases shares or when the number of shareholders exceeds the maximum allowed—resulting in large tax payment.

Partnerships that already exist. Only the LLC allows for partnership-style pass-through taxation of business profits while shielding all owners (rather than just limited partners in a limited partnership) from personal liability for corporate obligations.

Real estate holding businesses. When assets are sold or liquidated, C corporations with their shareholders are subject to a double tax on appreciation—taxation happens at both the corporate and individual levels. S corporations that were formed as C corporations may be liable to double taxation on gains from valued assets and a penalty tax on passive income (money from rents, royalties, interest, or dividends) if it exceeds a certain threshold. Because the LLC is a real pass-through tax form, it permits a company to avoid double taxes on appreciated assets. When a firm is sold, the proprietors, not the entity, often pay taxes on the sale gains.

Incorporating Success in your Business

Setting up a Limited Liability Company or LLC is one of the best options for you as you build the business side of your hotshot company. Forming an LLC gives you several advantages and safety nets as a business owner.

It shields you from personal liability and establishes a limited liability structure through the business. You will also be given a Federal Employer Identification Number, which functions similarly to a social security number for your company. If you want to open a bank account or conduct business with your state government, this will be required.

You are not required to file a corporate tax return; however, you will be required to file with your state. Creating a Limited Liability Company also gives you financial options such as a business, including lines of credit, loans, and business rate credit cards. These are based upon your Federal EIN and the credit you build through your Company.

Laws and fees vary by state, and you aren't even required to open the LLC in the state you reside or operate in. However, you are required to have a registered agent in that state.

You can form an LLC on your own by submitting paperwork to your state, but it is strongly recommended that you hire an attorney or a registration company to handle the paperwork. A lawyer will be more expensive than a registration company, so the final decision is yours. However, once your Limited Liability Company is formed, you must follow up with your state government regarding any additional fees or documents that must be filed.

Often, businesses will form an LLC in a state with lower taxes or fees, but you must have a physical address and someone working for you in that state. Many LLC registration companies will provide the registered agent, including it in the first-year filing fee.

Liability Protection

The LLC creates a shield for small business owners. These are not directly responsible for the company's debts and commitments. This legal entity also offers a single taxation layer that minimizes taxes on shareholders and allows active members to deduct from other incomes if the Company generates losses.

They are a popular business structure for small businesses because they offer flexibility, limited liability protection, and the possibility of a lower tax bill. This entity operates as a corporation in the state but is taxed like a partnership or sole proprietorship in the federal government. It provides its owners with the same limited liability protection as a corporation while avoiding double taxation by passing earnings through to the owners. When Limited Liability Company members pay their income taxes, they are taxed only once.

There are no restrictions on how many members it can have. These businesses do not require a board of directors or even multiple members. You can form a single-member LLC.

The process of forming one is straightforward. You can hire an agent to do it for you or apply at the state secretary's office. You'll have to pick a business name and file your articles of organization. This document is the governing rulebook for your Limited Liability Company. In the case of single-member LLCs, it isn't particularly important. However, you should have a lawyer draft this agreement with multiple members since it can have massive implications for your revenue split and other operational questions.

Along with your articles, you'll need to draft an operating agreement that details how you and your partners will run the LLC daily. One of the members is usually designated as the managing member and is in charge of the organization's operations. Many states do not require operating agreements, but it is a good idea to create one anyway in case of future disputes.

LLCs can hire employees; to do this; you'll need to apply for an EIN with the IRS. Once your agreement and articles have been filed with the state, some states will require you to post an ad in the newspaper announcing the formation of your Limited Liability Company. You'll have to check which publications are appropriate for this with the local county office.

Raising money is simple with an LLC, unlike sole props, even if it isn't as easy as a corporation. An investor becomes a member, not a shareholder since they can't issue shares themselves. While membership is a good option for new investors, it can get tricky to cash their money out (Zarzycki, 2020). I'll address this situation shortly.

The most appealing aspect of an LLC is that it protects its owners from liability while also allowing you to reduce your overall tax bill. When establishing one, you must open a separate bank account to hold the Company's funds. If you do not do this, you may expose your assets to liability litigation. In some states, if it is operated from your bank account, it is used as evidence that your assets are also involved in the litigation, and the LLC's protection is voided.

Income is not the end of security and taxes. The Limited Liability Company also allows business owners to change how they want to run and manage their company. You are not required to fit into a standard size that applies to all governance systems.

Business owners frequently build their companies without holding legal persons or complying with legal enforcement criteria. The legislation governing limited liability companies was specifically designed to encourage the use of this vehicle. A minimum requirement is the formation and management of a Limited Liability Company.

Another advantage is that a lawyer's corporation conveys a more professional and official profile. Customers understand that the company is a Limited Liability Company and that its founders took their work seriously. It's great to do more business.

So, when we ask what LLC stands for, we get the most common small business legal entity vehicle. A business owner receives numerous benefits and advantages in exchange for a low price.

Excellent Defense from Lawsuits

These business organizations can also protect a business owner from someone who wants to prosecute him. If you properly sign as management or a mere member, the organization can help you against any lawsuits. This likewise means that you do not insert your expenses into your company account and are running your bank account as a company. The courts will investigate how you independently run the company, which means they will check if the corporation is on its own two feet and has its accounts and expenses independent from the employees. If you have not deferred the company reports, you would be well-positioned to protect yourself from liability. This also means you have not committed fraud, as these institutions cannot defend you against fraud if you face a trial. If the opposing party demonstrates fraud, it quickly becomes the corporate veil.

LLC Taxation

Certainly, the LLC tax is distinct from corporate tax. The LLC S business policy helps reduce the self-employment tax or fully avoid it. You have all the usual business tax write-offs open to you. However, if you work solely under the corporate agency for your Company, you cannot escape a self-employment tax. You can look for an accountant and understand a corporate structure to mitigate self-employment tax.

An example of this is an S Company which pays you to form your Limited Liability Company. There is a lot of Limited Liability Company information about Internet taxes that you can find. Different tactics shift year by year; what appeals most to business owners to the concept of avoiding self-employment tax. Becoming an employee of your own company is the most sought technique.

Furthermore, your LLC pays for the establishment of a business. Paying a low income and thus paying large dividends reduces net tax even further. These techniques can be complex and necessitate extensive research and good CPA implementation.

It's fine to start operating with your LLC and earning more than an accountant in the early stages of your business. Forming a corporation at the state level is usually more expensive and necessitates more laws and regulations to ensure enforcement and corporate custody.

Profits, losses, deductions, and credits all pass through to your income, and you must include them all on your tax return at the end of the year. In addition, your LLC will be required to pay state income taxes and other business-related taxes, such as self-employment taxes. It is best to have them filed by an accountant.

Chapter 6. Common Mistakes to Avoid When Forming an LLC

Operating a small business is a challenging experience for even the most seasoned small business owners. Mistakes are common in business, so it is critical to learn from your mistakes. However, it is also beneficial to avoid making the same mistake. This chapter will address some of the most common LLC mistakes to help and guide you when forming and operating an LLC.

One of the most common mistakes is filing to become an LLC in the wrong state. Your geographic location may prevent you from any other option, but it needs to be considered. Some states have a better relationship with their LLC owners and treat them better than other states. This is also true for other business operations within the state.

It is recommended that you conduct some research before filing to form your LLC to determine whether your state has any strict or flexible business statutes. At the very least, this research will give you an idea of what your company is in for in the long run. The history of how your state treats small business owners will help you understand how current fees will change over time and what the tax obligation will look like in the future.

You should probably just file in your state if you're just starting a small LLC because all states value small business owners, some advantages that companies that do not incorporate will not have.

Not following through and understanding your company's legal obligations to conduct business in your state is a huge misstep. It is a common misconception that incorporating your business gives it legitimacy in the community.

Every business will still be required to obtain and maintain current business licenses for the community they operate. Depending on the nature of your business and the products or services you offer, you will need to obtain a business license or license to comply with local and state laws.

After you have become an official LLC and obtained all of your business licenses, there is the task of remaining an LLC in your state. Every state will have requirements you and your LLC must meet to comply with the LLC rules and regulations.

If you do not maintain your compliance as an LLC, you risk jeopardizing the protections for which you formed your LLC in the first place. If your safeguards are compromised, your assets may be vulnerable to litigation, and you may lose your business and personal financial stability.

There are several ways to stay compliant to protect your personal and business assets. The first is one in which many business owners struggle. Keep your funds separate from those used solely for your business.

Because there will be no co-mingling of accounts or funds, keeping your funds separate protects your assets by not allowing your funds to be accessed in litigation.

Another common blunder is failing to use your company name when signing business documents. Using your business title complicates the argument that your signature was done personally. The main reason for forming an LLC is to protect your assets from litigation, so keeping your company business and personal business separate will eliminate the appearance of conflict.

Follow all of your state's requirements to stay in compliance with the state and protect yourself and your company from losing the status of protection that comes with operating an LLC. Your state will require you to submit an annual report detailing your income and any legal actions you have taken.

These annual reports must be submitted by a specific deadline, and you must ensure that you meet those deadlines. You must file for foreign qualifications if you are filing from a different state. To avoid losing your in-compliance status, ensure that you meet the state's requirements in which you are filing.

To ensure that your company remains in compliance, you must stay up to date on any changes made in your state or the state where you file your paperwork to ensure that you have met all of the requirements. These modifications may impact the deadlines and due dates for various aspects of an LLC's formation and certification process.

One of the most common misconceptions among business owners is that an LLC will protect its company in any situation. While incorporating your company into an LLC will provide you with significant protection, it will not protect your company at all costs. If your company engages in unethical or illegal behavior, it may breach the security provided.

Finally, the most common mistake made by a small business owner is assuming that your Company is too small to effectively form an LLC or Corporation to protect any of the Company or your assets.

If you pay attention to current trends, you will notice that it is very common to file lawsuits to the right that may only be perceived as wrong by one customer. It is extremely prudent to keep your personal and business finances separate.

Assume you decide not to incorporate your company and instead run it as a sole proprietorship. In that case, you will jeopardize all of your assets and expose yourself and your partner's assets to litigation. You will most likely be working more than 80 hours per week to generate new business to make your business as successful as possible. However, you will need to devote some time to incorporating or forming an LLC.

You will then be able to modify the structure of your business in a much more effective and efficient way in the future.

Mistakes to Avoid When Setting Up or Enlisting

For decades, an LLC has been a reliable way to protect your assets from the liabilities associated with apartment rental property. State governments provide this defense to encourage investment, strengthen the economy, and benefit society.

Fortunately, one of the primary purposes of Company and LLC laws is to protect private investors from personal responsibility to support society and the general public. However, a business must operate following the LLC statutes to receive the security shield. People frequently make serious mistakes when setting up their LLC or enlisting the assistance of a discount legal document service, a paralegal, an accountant, or even an attorney who is not specialized in LLC preparation. (Although a tax accountant's services are of considerable value, they are generally not carried out from an asset security point of view).

1. Wait before a tenant claims an injury or has started civil proceedings against you. If the LLC does not exist until a tenant claims or takes legal action, you gain zero insurance for your assets if you then make the LLC. It never ceases to confuse me how many consumers panic and hurry to create an LLC after being sued. It's always too late at that point.

2. Suppose the rental property is not transferred to the LLC properly when the LLC is formed. An LLC provides its owners with asset security only when the LLC transfers and retains the underlying rental property. A major step is to use a Quitclaim Deed or Grant Deed, which must be carefully worded and legally notarized. Unfortunately, many people did this critical process independently instead of relying on a paralegal or document preparation service.

Errors or omissions will result in an unintentional and unnecessary reassessment of property tax in any detail if not done correctly. A reassessment caused by a previous customer who wanted to move his property without proper instructions can be very costly to reverse. In retrospect, the authors of these errors probably wished they had hired an experienced LLC lawyer from the start.

3. If the LLC bank account is not opened, all LLC businesses operate from this account. While some of my new customers have formed an LLC, all LLC banking transactions have been handled through their accounts or DBA. All LLC revenue must be deposited into the LLC account, and all LLC expenses paid from the LLC account must be reimbursed. If a lawsuit fails to distinguish LLC funds from personal funds, the LLC will be disqualified, allowing creditors to threaten and seize personal property. Rent checks must be made payable to the LLC and deposited in the LLC account. All costs, including but not limited to mortgage payments, insurance, taxes, and maintenance, must be covered by the LLC account. You can pay an LLC cost regularly with your own

money and then write an LLC check to repay yourself in an emergency. This, however, can be kept to a bare minimum. In addition, your LLC should be equipped with a credit/debit card for small property transactions. If you use an agency to collect rentals in your name, the agency must forward rental income to the LLC rather than to you directly.

4. Shape a business rather than build an LLC for your rental property. To save money, many people make the mistake of forming a company for their rental property without seeking legal advice. This is a bad idea because a company like an LLC does not always protect this type of business. Extra tax filings and formalities, such as required meetings and business minutes, are frequently included in corporations. Even if you later decide to be taxed as a business, you can request that the IRS treat your LLC as an S or C corporation by filing the appropriate forms. I've had several clients who paid a paralegal or legal document service to help them set up an LLC or a company. They only discovered significant issues later and sought legal aid as a result. They are deeply dissatisfied because they have paid a lot of money for

worthless or incorrect papers and franchise taxes and started from scratch.

5. If you have a Living Trust, you must ensure that your LLC becomes or is owned by your trust. I met several new customers who had not transferred their LLCs into a family trust. If they died before the matter was settled, the LLC and its assets would be scrutinized and not directed toward the heirs, as the trust is designed to do. This is another area where competent legal counsel is essential to ensure that your properties are protected from legal action, well-maintained, and not subject to probate or excessive property taxes. Many other mistakes can be avoided by hiring an experienced LLC lawyer. If you have decided to form an LLC, it is not prudent to ensure that it is properly formed and operated. The LLC is a legal entity. However, improper use jeopardizes the safeguards it can provide.

Chapter 7.   Benefits of LLC for Property Owners

One of the most difficult aspects of starting a real estate investment business, whether a partnership or a sole proprietorship, is how to structure it. It is important to protect yourself from personal liability by separating your finances from your professional life. In most cases, it is nice to consult a real estate lawyer to review the different options and determine which one is right for you. In California, an "S" corporation or LLC may be better suited to your corporation because they are "pass-thru" tax entities in which individual shareholders pay a personal income tax. A "C" corporation may require more complex organizations, a separate taxable entity. In both cases, a real estate lawyer can help you in this decision-making process.

Suppose you're going to run your business as a sole proprietorship. In that case, you don't legally need a business plan like you do if you're going to invest in a Limited Liability Company, but I would urge you to have one anyway. The difference between a sole proprietorship and LLC is that a Limited Liability Company is an established business in the government's eyes. It can be costly to start. However, it comes with several benefits, the biggest of which are the tax benefits and the protection it provides you in the case of a lawsuit. I urge you to look into getting an LLC rather than running your business as a sole proprietor.

A business plan is a document where you write down your business goals, how you intend to achieve them, and how long it will take you. A business plan also describes your company's nature, financial projections, and the steps you intend to take to achieve those projected goals.

It's important to have a business plan because it lays out your goals and the strategies you'll use to achieve them. Remember, you're laying out a strategy for success. You can effectively sit and spin your wheels until you run your business into the ground if you don't know your goals and how to get there. You are more likely to succeed if you have a clear action plan.

At the very least, it should include:

- A current budget.
- A three-year sales forecast.
- Sales and production strategy.
- Market analysis.
- Projected expense budget for three years connected to your current budget.
- A profit and loss statement.
- Break-even analysis
- Team outline (strengths and how to deal with their weaknesses/ manage them).
- SWOT (strengths, weaknesses, opportunities, and threats relating to your business).
- Product and/or services summary.
- Mission statement.
- Vision statement.

If you're writing up a plan for people to invest in your company, you'll also need an income projection. It's not necessary, however, if the plan is just for yourself.

When developing your plan, consider how much money you need to make to reach certain business milestones, where you are now, and how you will get from where you are to where you want to be. You will also need to determine the best way to reach your target market. There are numerous marketing strategies to choose from; you must be astute in determining which strategy is most effective for your target market. It is also beneficial to cultivate relationships with other small business owners to contract when you need work done.

Every business is different. The approaches to selling products and services differ depending on what kind of business you have. And those approaches will also differ per product or service. You need a strategy for each, and your business plan is the way to achieve that.

You may have different divisions that fall under the umbrella of your brand. It is normal to use a different marketing strategy for each division. For example, you may have a home renovation aspect to your brand and the investment division. The marketing strategies you will use to attract renovation projects differ from your strategy for expanding your investment portfolio.

Real Estate Tax Strategies and Forming an LLC

If you plan to travel from New York City to San Francisco, you will see good road signs that will help you find your way without needing a detailed road map.

The same applies when you decide to invest in the business. If you have a clear picture of the benefits and advantages of different kinds of real estate deals, assess your current position in terms of resources, and move in the right direction with the least amount of wasted time, it will be a major asset to you. This chapter's goal is to help you see where you are, where you want to go, and the best way to get there.

The first thing you should do is go over your current financial evaluation. Is your credit good or bad? Do you have access to money lending avenues? Are private and public lenders ready to help you get started?

Once you have examined your current status, you are ready to start selecting the right kind of deals to push you towards financial freedom. For instance, if you have smaller credit resources, you will want to select real estate deals that do not depend on credit or funding.

Property Types and Investment Approaches

Real estate investing is a great option because there are so many different types of properties to invest in and techniques for what to do with those properties. And each has its own set of benefits.

Investors weigh various options based on the outcome they want to achieve, the amount of money they want to put into the project, and their level of experience with various strategies.

For example, an investor may prefer quick cash investment methods for various reasons, such as a lack of working capital or high consumer debt.

Multiple income streams and opportunities necessitate specialized knowledge in various areas.

Multiple Income Streams

You could be wondering how to select your income streams and what factors should dictate your decision. Here's a list of the different types of income:

- Wholesaling.
- Probate.
- Remodeling.
- Rehabbing.
- Land development.
- Discount note selling.
- Foreclosures.
- Meanwhile, here are some passive streams of income in real estate:
- Leases.
- Property management.
- Recreational parks.
- Rentals.
- Apartment houses.
- Mobile home parks.

In general, anything you will contract and sell quickly falls into earned income.

Passive income refers to money that you get week after week or monthly without going out and making/closing another deal. As a result, passive income is sometimes called a recurring income.

For real estate, properties that fall under passive income streams are your buy-and-hold rentals. Once you close on these deals, you collect rent every single month. Another real estate field that can be considered passive is when you become a property manager or own a property management company. Investors use you to collect the rents and pay you some fee for doing it.

Portfolio Income

Here is when your money starts to generate more money for you, especially through interest.

There are different ways to generate portfolio income that is real estate related. Most of these income methods relate to investors earning interest on their money.

Types of Streams of Portfolio Income in Real Estate

Real estate can help investors build wealth in a systematic, compounding manner.

While everyone is different and has different time demands and goals, professional real estate investors will always want to have 3-5 streams of earned income and 2-3 streams of portfolio income.

New investors with a limited amount of money start by being knowledgeable in various earned income streams like foreclosure, wholesale, and rehabbing. They now have a lot of control over their ability to generate large sums of money in a short time. They then take that money and begin investing in real estate, buying, and holding.

As the passive income or lease option properties grow, the investor has two options: buy another buy and hold property or invest in a portfolio stream.

Distressed Properties vs. Motivated Sellers

An old saying about real estate investing goes, "There are only two types of deals out there, distressed properties or distressed sellers."

You will realize that certain properties have a higher ideal investment opportunity than others, no matter your investment strategy. Professional investors evaluate each deal against a set of criteria, considering the benefits of that type of deal versus the opportunities available. They do not always exhibit all the characteristics listed, but they assess and make well-informed decisions.

When evaluating a distressed property, look for the following advantages:

- They have minimal competition because the average individual wants properties in the best condition.
- You can always buy distressed properties under flexible, easy terms and prices relatively below the market value.
- You have the freedom to heighten the value through smaller improvements and rehab work.
- A lot of market areas have many distressed properties to select from.

Some things to consider about distressed properties include:

1. Many real estate markets have a certain number of investors searching for this type of property, so your marketing efforts should be active, well-organized, and effective to discover better deals. It can be great to investigate different marketing strategies well for other real estate investors.

2. To avoid costly mistakes, you must know how to examine the property and neighborhood accurately.

3. Through inspections and repairs, estimates have to be done before the purchase.

4. If the property is in a low-income neighborhood, comparable sales in that area will exceed a certain amount of money, regardless of how the change is made. Repairs are usually expensive. To maximize profitability in older, lower-income areas, it is safe to combine a distressed property with a distressed seller and maximize profit potential in all aspects.

Meanwhile, here are the pros of working with distressed sellers:

− In each price range, there is seller distress. Property can sometimes be purchased in flexible and simple terms. The seller requires assistance and, in most cases, simply wants a way out but is unsure what to do. You can provide a solution.

− When you can connect a distressed seller with a distressed property, you have a great opportunity to increase property value through cosmetic changes.

You must determine what caused the seller's situation and the best way to assist them in escaping it. You must develop good listening and negotiation skills to understand their problem and find the best solution.

Certain distressed sellers provide compelling reasons for wanting to stay in their properties, which tends to accommodate this. This can be risky if their problem is financial. It is important to keep your emotions at bay.

Purchasing as Wholesale

Distressed properties are the best option for wholesaling candidates, and wholesaling is a great opportunity because it requires the least expertise and is the kind of deal new investors want.

Because you have a good chance of finding distressed properties, wholesale deals may be one of the first types of deals you make in real estate investing.

To be successful in wholesaling, you must understand how to segment your market correctly, create a database of potential properties, and many other things. You must also understand a few fundamental aspects of the wholesale business, such as:

1. Analyzing Prospects

Because distressed properties should be your main target, you must learn to identify and review distressed homes. You should also understand that a distressed property does not necessarily imply a good deal but rather a great starting point. As a result, you must memorize the techniques that will assist you in determining when a deal is too good to be true, when it is appropriate to proceed, and when the deal should be abandoned.

2. Computing the Market Value

To succeed as a wholesaler, you must know the significance of calculating fair market value after repairs. The real estate experts on your power team will be valuable assets for finding this information. Also, using comparable sales of properties in the same location will allow you to know the market value.

3. Estimating Repairs

This will not work if you do not accurately estimate repairs. Learn how to check deals to ensure that you present an offer that will result in the greatest profit. You can also learn techniques to help you save money on rehab projects while increasing your profits.

4. Submitting Offers and Counteroffers

You have to become familiar with good communication and negotiating skills, learn how to submit offers and counteroffers without destroying your goals, and learn how to manage contracts. Understanding how to review properties properly will be significant in determining what to offer and whether you need to make an offer.

5. Getting Buyers

Wholesaling is only half done when you find deals and bargains but have no one to assign contracts to. Creating a large investor database to tap into, regardless of the type of deal you're working on, will help you move things along quickly while maintaining your profit margins.

How to Close Effectively

You must learn the right ways to close without money.

Lease Options

Leases are one of the most appealing real estate investment opportunities for both new and experienced investors because they can generate multiple income streams from a single transaction. Here are some general points you need to know about lease options in real estate; if you purchase a property using a lease option, you can:

- Engage with distressed sellers rather than distressed properties. The seller's circumstances create the deal. What you must do is identify the owner's issues.
- Acquire freedom of a property without taking ownership. You are not required to buy, but you have earned the right to do so.
- Manage beautiful homes in beautiful settings. In this case, the seller must exit, and the investor must enter. Demand rises as the neighborhood improves.
- Help someone in a variety of ways. The most distinguishing feature of lease options is always debt relief. You are constantly dealing with people who do not want to sell their property but are forced due to financial constraints. Thus, you can help someone find a solution quickly. Likewise, you can do it with or without money.

Foreclosures

The foreclosure market can be a great channel for making a profit for new and experienced investors. Foreclosures occur daily, and this could be your opportunity to make a wise investment and assist someone in need.

Keep in mind that foreclosures can happen for various reasons, and this is a niche where you can achieve a win-win scenario and do something that assists both you and the individual in need. Investors must negotiate well with lenders and homeowners to boost profits on these deals.

With so many different strategies and ways to make money in real estate, knowledge will be essential for success.

You will have completed your first critical step toward financial independence by reviewing the available opportunities in real estate investing. It's time to move on to the next level.

Conclusion

Limited Liability Companies are popular due to the elements that allow the corporation and the partnership to work together. For example, when signing up for an LLC, you eliminate some of the negatives of being a Corporation or a Partnership alone. The LLC will provide limited liability to the owners and the shareholders and offers a pass-through income tax rate.

The benefits can be more advantageous because it provides more flexibility to business owners, resulting in an agreement for operating based on the owners' needs and requirements. It provides limited liability for the members or shareholders by holding the company liable for its debts and liabilities. It benefits the LLC because it is not taxed at the corporate level. Instead, it permits the Company's losses on their returns to be passed on to individual shareholders. Finally, it assists the Company in avoiding double taxation, allowing them to keep profits within the Company for future growth.

However, there are several disadvantages to the LLC. One of those disadvantages is the pass-through tax status. The losses and profits are reported on the individual's tax returns, which can be unfavorable if the shareholders receive some dividends. Due to the LLC structure, the investors may be hesitant to invest or loan money to the company. You also may find that you have more taxes or fees associated with the LLC. There is a required upfront cost in some states that initially costs higher. These states require the LLC to pay a franchise or capital values tax, often based on revenue, owners, and profitability.

Made in the USA
Middletown, DE
16 October 2023

40935486R00057